WARSCAPE
WITH LOVERS

CSU Poetry Series LII

Marilyn Krysl

War–
scape
with
Lovers

for Nancy,
long time friend
in the art of poetry.
affectionately
Marilyn Krysl

Cleveland State University Poetry Center

ISBN: 1-880834-28-6 (paper)
         1-880834-29-4 (cloth)
Library of Congress Catalog Card Number: 97-65396

First Printing
Published by the Cleveland State University Poetry Center
1983 East 24th Street, Cleveland, OH 44115-2440
Manufactured in the United States of America

Funded Through
Ohio Arts Council

727 East Main Street
Columbus, Ohio 43205-1796
(614) 466-2613

Acknowledgments

Grateful acknowledgment is made to the following publications in which some of these poems first appeared.

ANOTHER CHICAGO MAGAZINE: Ghazals 1 through 8 of "Ghazals for the Turn of the Century"

DENVER QUARTERLY: "Homage to Pierre Auguste Renoir"

KANSAS QUARTERLY: "Water" and "Blazon"

KENYON REVIEW: "Suite for Kokodicholai, Sri Lanka"

LOUSIVILLE REVIEW: "Batticaloa: Staying Alive"

PRAIRIE SCHOONER: "Free Trade Zone: Shirmala's Pneumonia," "Venture Capital," "Famine Relief"

RED DIRT: "Ghazal #9

VISIONS INTERNATIONAL: "Eden of Water"

SPOON RIVER POETRY REVIEW: "Poem for Extraordinary Day"; "Carpe Diem: Time Piece" received the *Review's* 1995 Award for Poetry

WOMEN'S REVIEW OF BOOKS: "Warscape with Lovers"

The University of Colorado and the Colorado Council on the Arts and Humanities funded research on which some of these poems are based. I also wish to thank friends who were especially helpful: Robin Becker, Jonathan Holden, Mary Crow, Alicia Ostriker, Hilda Raz, Reg Saner, Carolyn Beard Whitlow, and Renata Wood.

Contents

I: WAR

Nammu: To Adam

The sea keeps sending my emissaries, wave
upon light filled wave inscribed with my name,
as though you call me and call me, and I hear and come
and come. I am walking toward you, a torch
in my hand, lengths of light, shaft after burning
shaft: your lit face. You sit in the midst

of immense love, not alone. You sit in the midst
of this going and coming and going. Love is a wave,
a verb moving through the moments. Cut to the burning
hut, the woman fleeing with her child: my name
here for a moment, then gone. Then water, my torch
coming toward you again. A time will come

when I'll come for you. We'll go. A time will come
because time does that. Over and over in the midst
of love there is war: women, and men with torches,
orders to burn the village. Meanwhile, the wave
swells: etched on its curve, my foaming name:
the sound of water rising like a god, burning

across the air, dispersing. Rising, burning
and again dispersing. I am time, come
around you like an egg. Rejoice! Your faltering name
will dissolve into mine: even in the midst
of uttering these flaming words, another wave
flings down the names of the thousands dead. No torch

can consume the sea: you cry out, in fear. A torch
for light, yes, and another brand for burning
the enemy's fields. Where one wave ends a wave
begins: I am love's azure, woman coming
out of the water, a curve of spray. In the midst
of your prayer, the woman beside you utters my name

and you turn, see me. The beloved. Ask me to name
the ones I've loved. Adam, there are many torches,
more dead than you can count. Now, in the midst

of love, a mass of darkness. I lift the burning
skull, so you will understand. Come,
kiss me. You are mostly light, and water, a wave

of flesh. My name, burning your lips. You
have been a torch in the midst of a wave of destruction.
Your shroud of water is ready. Come with me.

Water

I, the Glittering One, of silvery body
    and gliding, a series of moments seemingly liquidly
        infinite, who, when you want me, willingly answer
            gratis, slick with myself, supple and immediate,

I who have brought you oracular orchards, damp gardens,
    lakes set with bridges and lanterned pavilions,
        who manifest, fine mist at the sea's surface,
            glittering amidst young shoots of spring wheat.

Maker of froth, of the filigree surge of fountains,
    lapping and harboring the thrust of peninsular cities,
        scattering my emeralds among the emirates, prostrate,
        offering the populace my slippery bounty,

soothing the sick beds of your rivers by lying in them,
    tenderly attending your morning and evening ablutions,
        I, who make a tinkling music as I go from you,
            who tease you out to the tip of your own tongue,

I who have been your happy slave, endlessly
    attentive, endlessly available, I will say it now:
        you have used me badly. I who was The Infinitely
        Wet One, listen to me now: I am very thirsty.

Suite for Kokodicholai, Sri Lanka

1. Daughter

My mother's name was Mamangam Maheswary
We thought many together would be safe
When you're afraid, a crowd seems good
I believed in the mill I could hide my children

My mother sat down in the center of the room
Her sari was red, the color of heat
The rest of us scurried like rats   She was calm
The soldiers' shouts sounded like shots

I pushed my children back, behind the others
My mother's back the spine of a queen
Like an old tree she had grown strong
I have seen grown men tremble in her presence

But these soldiers were not men, nor am I woman
Like a rat I hid beneath my dead children
My mother sat like a stone carving
Her full name was Mamangam Maheswary

2. Husband

I was in my fields when I heard the first shots
I walked quickly   The houses were empty
I could hear the soldiers ahead, firing
Then I met others, also walking quickly

We came to Kumaranayagam's mill
Beside the gate red blossoms of hibiscus
The gate stood open   Beyond I saw my wife
She stood in the compound as though she owned nothing

Inside a strip of light lay across the floor
A woman knelt dipping a cloth in a bucket
Again and again she washed the same stain
The stain began to gleam, as though polished

My wife had laid our children side by side
She had placed the smallest between the other two
She had laid the boy between his two sisters
They liked to walk that way, one on either side

3. *Wife*

After the mine the soldiers came
Among those men they took was my husband
They made the men circle the crater three times
Then the soldiers forced them into the center

The third one herded in was my husband
Where I stood I could see his face as they shot him
I watched as one by one the others fell
Their bodies one above the other, sticks of wood

I have seven children   I know my husband's body
After the burning I did not know his body
After the burning I did not see his face again
This cloth is a piece of his sarong, partly burned

Bank: Colombo

Where the road wound down toward the sea
they cordoned off. The length that was the Green
is leveled dirt. That blackened steel's the bank.
The hotel windows, boarded up, look mean.

Only the sea still flings its cries into
the air, the way it did when we walked by.
The bomb was made abroad: someone paid cash.
People say *I couldn't even cry.*

We gave away our cash and thought this kind.
You said you loved me. How blind with need
we were, like this country. Above the sand
two wings, a single gull. The place feels numb:
no gods here. I know the feel of stone.
See that stone? Stones lie where they were flung.

Batticaloa: Staying Alive

I write this now as a way of honoring
these days, and the way we move through them,
because we live near the end of the world,
men on the streets with rifles, men at checkpoints,

trucks moving in men, and women, with rifles.
Sometimes soldiers make house to house searches,
or they sweep the paddy fields for guerrillas,
cut the throats of fishermen or a priest.

Sometimes a girl from the high school
doesn't come home. The jaggedness of lightning
fits our nerves perfectly. Men go to work,
women buy rice and oil at the market, children

call to each other across the air
as though diurnal day were indestructible,
though tossing that shout toward the sky
could be the last thing they ever do.

All this in heat that comes like a giant being,
bearing huge blossoms in its hands.
All you can do is walk to the sea, lie down
in the bosom of water. Coming back at evening,

the suasion of ocean was in me, its blue riff
of languor, of urgency, and the enormous light
went on lowering itself slowly
into the deepening colors of the world.

I walked beneath fringes of banana leaves,
past the camp, past shops, past the checkpoint,
that bunker where two soldiers leaned out watching,
light from their eyes an arc of desire

looking for its one, right place in the dark.
Sometimes, when the light deepens and fills
like water rising to the rim of a basin,
we rise up out of our single silence

and become gods. Evening, a child cries,
a woman stirs something in a pot
because when they've carried away the dead
those who are left will want to eat. When dark

comes and you're alive, you want to kiss
the beggar at the gate, the crippled clerk,
the general who knew about the disappearances
and let them go on. You open, ripe fruit

easily coming loose from its stone,
and those waves keep passing the light through space
finally into the mass of the earth. You left
the other men at the table, rising like light

on its way to the next world. In a dry place
the pealing of water is many bells at once.
You knelt, unfastened my sandals, and I stepped
from the dust this body is made of into the aria

of your hands. Friend, my heel in your palm
was a thing one person could not do alone.
What you must say at the end is yes:
if this is the moment of death, then this

is the altar of water, and this one before me now
is the other. Here are my hands, here the feet
of the beloved. This anointing
is what is true, now, here in this country.

Summer Solstice, Batticaloa, Sri Lanka

The war had turned inward until it resembled
suicide. The only soothing thing was water.
I passed the sentries, followed the surf out of sight.
I would sink into the elements, become simple.

Surf sounds like erasure, over and over.
I lay down and let go, the way you trust an animal.
When I opened my eyes, all down the strand
small crabs, the bright yellow of a crayon,

had come out onto the sand. Their numbers, scattered,
resembled the galactic spill and volume of the stars.
I, who had lain down alone, emptied,
waked at the center of ten thousand prayers.

Who would refuse such attention. I let it sweeten me
back into the universe. I was alive, in the midst
of great loving, which is all I've ever wanted.
The soldiers of both sides probably wanted just this.

Warscape with Lovers

Scent of plumeria, and the smell of burning.
Not one or the other, but both. Destruction, and the blossom.
Sweetheart, I'm afraid. That boy with the rifle breaks
the catechism in two. And in two. Let me
see us whole, beside the sea. My body
busy, paying attention to yours. Already

we rock each other with our voices. Already
we're braiding the invisible cord. That burning
hut on T.V. isn't ours, but could be. My body
could be hers, child at dead breast. That blossom
of blood and bone could be your face. Let me
say truth: no place, no one, is safe. The breaking

of vows, we know, is a given. Sweetheart, you'll break
my heart. I've broken yours, but look: already
you love me again. Destruction and the blossom: let me
say it another way: that soldier, burning
to become fabulous, torches the thatch (see blossomy
flame) of the enemy's hospital: cut to my body,

clay taking shape in your hands. Body by body,
war piled on war: when will the heart break
all the way open? Thunder of mortar, blossom
in the gutter. The soldier firing the mortar already
dead. This is how we live: running from the burning
field, into each other's arms. Let me

lie along your side. Give me something to hold. Let me
ride those waves pouring from your fingers. The bodies
of the disappeared toll like bells. Our koan burns:
it cannot be solved. The whole and the broken,
dream and nightmare: your hand in my hair, already
familiar, could be the torturer's. Vase and its blossoms

camouflage for the bomb. You love where you can. *Blossom*
means lovely, full of promise. That's us: now let me
let this moment go. Our glass, half full—already

there's more—swells toward the rim. Ours the bodies
the death squads passed by. The refugees make a break
for the fence, running for their lives, crossing this burning,

broken, blossoming Century. They've already paid
our dues. Sweetheart, let me show you how: hand
on the body's book—now swear the burning vow.

Blazon

How say you're sexy oh my centerfold!
The coral is boiling, and the carcasses of flamingos

How say *the pillars of your thighs*
The hummingbird is on its last legs

How say *the mighty shield of your torso*
Ivory of elephants, tusks stacked in piles

And how shall I describe your eyes, my beloved
Eyes that cast the glittering net of heat over my body

If I look in your eyes I will see myself there
and behind me

    the shipments of dolphin calls
    the shipments of eagle wings
    the shipments of hills, lakes, clouds

II: GHAZALS FOR THE TURN OF THE CENTURY

They enter into darkness
who worship ignorance,
into greater darkness
those who delight in knowledge.
                    —Isa Upanishad

1

—*The elephant, bound, thinks longingly of the elephant grove.*

                              —The Hinayana

Look: see the peasant blasted at his crop.
The refugees kidnapped, made to carry ammunition.

The missiles dismantled, rebuilt, reinstalled.
The carcinogenic apples, the bereft gorilla mother.

The Vietnam vet propped against plate glass.
The six-year-old girl, the photographs of the body.

Friend phones long distance, love affair going badly.
I've forgotten the word for the double bladed axe.

Meanwhile the sky goes on with its watercolor.
Leaves, gorgeous, fall. The baby cries to be fed.

I feed the baby, watch the sky do its masterpiece.
The peasant again, rice green, his face burst open.

2

Flying over the heads of strangers—is this strafing?
In the museum with his father the boy admires armor.

The gorget, the lancerest, the loinguard, the breastplate
beneath which the heart pumps, the heart longs.

Look: see the seventy different kinds of daggers!
See how the headpiece stuns with its brightness!

Now think Whitman. Grandeur, think westward expansion,
the planet a sphere. Boots, guns, the fast car,

quick now, the necktie, the shot glass, the bar graph,
the radar screen, the printout of the body count—

How this energy cries out for use, satisfaction!
Bam. The young brave knocked from his pony.

Bam. The guerrilla, a spasm in foliage.
Now the woman, babe at her breast. Bam bam bam.

3

Watch my chic black. I attract the damaged man.
He sees a deep breast, a spring of milk.

He thinks if he touches me, if I let him touch me,
his hands will heal, he will play the piano again,

and his feeling, boarded up in rage,
will come forth and stand in the light, upright.

He imagines the water, its hands, their balm.
He imagines the queen in her fat honeycomb.

I take the first plane to the other side of the world.
When I arrive, he's there, waiting.

He thinks love heals, he thinks I am the healer.
He imagines the damaged can repair one another.

4

The men, the famous, fascinating men. Where are they?
And their scintillant wives, the printouts of the figures.

Are they breathing the carbon monoxide in the coke plant?
Do they work the mines, build the silicate molds?

Can they breathe? Can they work? Can they stand up?
Can they keep down food? Can they work again tomorrow?

Kick a chair, smash bottles in the street, stone cars.
Drown a cat. Hold down a girl. Hold down a girl.

Was she beautiful? Joyful? Was she mouthy? Was she handy?
Was it something to do? Was it just for the hell of it?

Would you do it again, if you could get away with it?
Have you done it again? How many times have you done it?

5

In hell children work. Chittagong is in hell,
El Paso, Lahore, Marrakech, Bahrain, you name it.

Don't stop to urinate, don't stop to eat,
pain with the thousand teeth, keep going,

Cairo, the camel races, boys sold for jockeys.
Colombo: boys and girls, the tourist beaches.

The blowing of glass, the harvesting of coffee,
leather goods, brass locks, factories producing matches,

fifteen cents a day, fifteen hours without a break,
New Delhi, Mirzapur, Islamabad, while in Bern

the executive sips cappucino, makes a phone call.
Imagination, said Joubert, *is the eye of the soul.*

6

The man's body is sacred and the woman's body is sacred.
The new death camp at Ketziot, no water.

The farmer, plowing, uncovers the burials.
He digs out the bones, sells the ancestors to tourists.

See how the deaths of the animals surround us.
How the carcasses mount, furs pile in the warehouse.

The sweatshop saw, the boy's hand on the floor.
Let us abandon then our gardens and go home.

The tricked self waits, biting its fingernails,
cut away from earth, adrift in a capsule, weightless,

the tricked self, blind in its little darkness,
outside history, breathing air from a can.

What have we done, my people, with the blazing gift?
The rites, songs, vows, the sacred initiations?

The beings of the future: those who ache to be born.
The beings of the future: what shall we say to them?

7

Plato, on beauty: *And coming to earth, we find her,*
coming to earth, we find her here too, shining.

Has she left us then, in shame and disgust?
Has she walked into the gracious, accepting waters?

Upright citizen, do you honor the Imperishable?
Where can I buy one? How many are there? How much are they?

Where are the smart with their grants, their credentials?
We do not know how to clean the water, fix a stem.

See the child's skull, broken open.
See the mountains bent double in pain.

Sky turns away, pulls its winding sheet around it.
The animals turn away. Their sorrow is not for us.

This is your face, and this is the child's body.
This is not what you wanted, but it is what you have done.

8

The self is nothing so small as a fist, but we experiment:
clip it, starve it, sear it, peel it, sew it shut.

Secretly we hope for a miracle. Presto.
Bring it now please, enlightenment. I'm ready.

The right therapeutic insight, the right discipline,
the right book, the right drug, the right combination,

not this failure to focus, this inability to act,
the waking in the night, the uncontrollable crying.

Seize new rhetoric: pain merely chemical interaction.
(Whose is the voice sobbing? Is it yours? Is it mine?)

We will do it, if we have to kill them to do it.
We will do it, if we have to kill ourselves to do it.

9

Bikini, 1953

A man came to our island. He came in a great ship.
He had many men. He said they needed our island.

He said Pack your belongings. We did not know what to do.
We did as he said. We did not know why.

The day they took us away no one ate any food.
The day they took us away no one ate any food.

When we looked back we saw the sea rise up.
Came then a great wave boiling across the water.

And the sky above the sea they darkened and burned.
They took us to an island where the water was bad.

Now we are no longer kind to each other.
I grieved for my garden, for the boat I had to leave.

In my last days there is no happiness.
In my last days I cannot go home.

10

The Palestinian boy throws rocks at the Israeli soldier.
The Israeli soldier beats up the Palestinian boy.

What is the self, this hypothetical piece of turf?
Perhaps after all it does not wear skirts.

Perhaps after all it does not wear a tie,
has no keys, no checkbook. No desire to own a mortgage.

Doesn't care which brand relieves cold symptoms sooner.
Does not desire a faster, sexier compact.

Does not wear a badge, does not carry a weapon,
does not plant flags on hillsides said to be captured.

The self is not a square, a rectangle, a pentagon.
The self is neither a circle nor a sphere.

The self exceeds the boundary of the single ego,
the genus, the family, the class order phylum,

includes the home court and the enemy battalion,
includes both sides and the border between them.

Includes the others: animal, vegetable. Mineral.
Includes the other colors, shapes, the other genitals.

Meanwhile here stand the frightened, and we are many.
When the earth burns, the frightened will inherit the earth.

11

When they shaved my head, I agreed I deserved it.
When they shaved me below, I agreed I deserved it.

They took the money for drugs. I told the girl, No bread.
They took the money for guns. I told the boy, Go to work.

Nor did I question the accidents, the disappearances,
though by then I knew they were lying.

Then they came for me, they held my head under water.
They let me breathe. They held me under again.

Three held me down while the others hurt me.
Look: here they carved their names on my body.

They made me dig, go in the hole, lie down.
They filled the hole. They piled on stones.

This is the place. You are in the presence of gods.
Don't lie. When you lie the gods have to wait.

The books have been burned. There are no instructions.
This is the bottom. Proceed without instructions.

12

for Hedda Nussbaum, 1989

Black is the color of my true love's hair
Black is the color of her face, its torn flap

Black is the color of my hands, fallen off
Black is the color of his teeth, fallen out

Black is the color of his mouth as he eats
Black is the color of her orphan name between his teeth

Black is the color of the first day I let him hurt her
Black is the color of the first day I helped him hurt her

Black is the color of the last day I helped him hurt her
Black is the color of the bathroom floor, the water

Black is the color of the days that stretch behind me
Black is the color of the days that stretch before me

Black is the color of *now*, this moment
Black my charred heart at the center of this moment

13

Find the still point: the reclining nude wakes.
Find the still point: the self stands, tries the lock.

No alarm screams, no siren deafens.
The rectangle swings open on its well oiled hinges.

No guard, no torturer, no bureaucrat, no minister,
no gang of toughs, no burglar, no mugger,

no father of drownings, no dead child of the father,
no crowd of men waiting their turn on her,

no squads, no platoons, no rifles, no bayonets,
no heads on poles, no breasts in piles,

no young ones in ditches burned with gasoline.
No hillsides of skeletons. No pits bulldozed over.

As I would not be a slave, so I would not be a master.
As I would not be a slave, so I would not be a master.

You have knocked on the door, wanting to know reasons.
Look: you have been knocking from the inside.

Rite

That is perfect. This is perfect. Perfect comes from perfect.
Take perfect from perfect, the remainder is perfect.

She is coming up, she is rising, she is coming
She is bearing aloft the waters in her water jars

She is coming up, she is rising, she is coming
She is bringing a bag of seed for the stony ground

She is coming up, she is rising, she is coming
She is setting the four winds in the four stars

She is coming up, she is rising, she is coming
She is bearing fire on its spool, the flame unwound

She is coming up, she is rising, she is coming
She is kneeling down before the holy number seven

She is coming up, she is rising, she is coming
She is cultivating the dark with her silver hoe

She is coming up, she is rising, she is coming
She is yoking the oxen of the sun to their burden

She is coming up, she is rising, she is coming
She is lying down like water in the fertile row

She is coming up, she is rising, she is coming
She is coming up, she is rising, she is coming
She is coming up, she is rising, she is coming

That is perfect, this is perfect, perfect comes from perfect.
Take perfect from perfect, the remainder is perfect.

15

The nude strides toward us. She is polished marble, walking.
This is the way light travels the universe.

You don't see her? Switch off the instrument panel.
Put down the knife. Don't put food in death's mouth.

Open your hand: the fist disappears.
Don't pick up the key. I repeat: don't pick up the key.

Give things away. Don't put food in death's mouth.
While you sleep on the train thieves put the money back.

Listen: learn the long prayers of the wind.
Shui Shih Ta: Speak to stones, to water.

Be a full bucket pulled up from darkness.
Come forward. Love something. Do you see her now?

16

Credo

We shall not shame one while the others watch
We shall not set ourselves against each other

We shall not bind ourselves together in a man's name
We shall not set ourselves against those far from us

nor set the men against the women and children
the creatures that run, fly, swim, or those rooted

What does the other smell like, sound like, feel like
How does she taste when you put your lips to her skin

Every day you put your lips to the skin of water
Every day you take the light as your lover

The highest form of goodness is like water.
It flows downward, through the lowest land, into. the sea.

17

Tell me, the poet said, what do you plan to do
with your one wild and precious life?

Every day I bless the water, drink the water.
Every day a stranger knocks asking for work.

Every day I give him work, every day I work beside him.
No more satisfying work than work with no purpose.

In the evening we eat the melons of twilight.
While we talk, another joins us.

The third one is the one who plays the flute.
The third one is the one who lies between us.

When the third one lies between us, we become one body.
There is no sweetness like the sweetness of the body.

In the dream I'm in a cavern, lit by one torch.
I raise the pick, hack the mineral wall.

I swing the pick again, break open a vein.
It is this gleaming that becomes dawn.

III: CALCUTTA

Kali Temple, Morning:
Crossing the Thoroughfare

Goddesses and gods ring the air, hailing us,
    consecrating our presence, those of us chosen,
        one more time, to wear the body's garment: each
          a prayer, rising like steam from the ground

at dawn. I go among this human cacophony,
    through clarion blare of motor and horn,
        and there, manifest in the air, you appear, child
          androgenous with nakedness, where I need

to cross. I am chosen, touched by a little god:
    winged heeled guide, you take hold. On the instant
        we become each other's courage. Our flared daring
          opens the stunned traffic, and we burn through,

smoke curling from incense, drift round a rickshaw,
    pause for a bus, wend, narrowly, between
        lorries, and where before there'd been nothing: a bike,
          gunned by a woman in sari. Her helmet's black:

we lean back from her wake, then ride the tide
    to shore, the crowd just more of our own teeming
        arrival. Wrapped in your gleaming godhead
          you let go, flit off to the rest of your life,

one moment falling into the next behind you,
    and I turn from our unison, denizen in your nation,
        pass stalls where women flick their bright needles,
          stringing garlands for the throat of Kali.

In deep humility before your gift to me,
    I wear this gilded vesture up through morning.
        I am clay, burnished by your generous impulse,
          glaze lit by your azure passage through my life.

Free Trade Zone: Shirmala's Pneumonia

Each intake of breath
another heave up
of a hammer. Then
she has to let it

go. Terror: error
could come at any
moment, and her own
body, that fakir,

make a fatal mistake,
and like a pump
seize up. Nothing
she can do about that.

This is a job
for one and only.
This is the scam
of low pay labor,

the helpless worker
who cannot choose
not to, who, menial,
must do for master,

and who am I, to be
whole and free,
one of the idle rich
who only watch?

Here comes fear, that
mugger, and I,
bystander, do not lift
a finger, but stand,

stunned onlooker,
at outer edge
of shadow circle
cast by interloper

Death: I merely
attend, in awe,
this great work
Breath

Famine Relief

Explain, please, this wonder, this
creaturous pleasure,

this ruby of feeling
while I feed another being: tell me why

when Hasina opens her mouth,
it's as though the world in its entirety

opens, the lotus of Buddha unfolding
its jewel. Veil of skin, draped over

bone: Hasina's fourteen, so thin
she can't walk, sit up,

hold a cup. Eyes a single beam
scanning for food, even when

she's full. She's the mouth
of the soul, open

around hunger, asking
the way a baby, without guile,

is good with greediness
to know the world. To feed another being

is like eating: both of us
filling ourselves

with the certainty that there is,
in us and around us,

kindness so infinite
that we cannot be lonely. Hasina

might have been the one with the spoon,
fleshy, of substantial body,

I the skeleton—but that too would be
wrong. Under the pull of full sun

at noon, I hear the temple
gong, summoning the faithful,

and in the lull of echo,
the jangle of bells on the women's

ankles. Hasina looks up,
I lift the spoon, balancing the pans

of our scale: ours
is a life of satiety

and hunger, the haves and the have nots,
these two conditions

spread through the universe
so that we may know hunger,

so that we may learn
to feed each other. Not perfection

but the lesson, enacted over
and over again: Hasina and I

by chance or quantum design,
chosen to perform this hallowed, ancient

devotion—one the Venus of Willendorf,
each of those many breasts

overflowing, the other Kali
in her starved aspect,

shrill around emptiness,
and devouring, devouring.

Venture Capital

I've rinsed Uma off, rubbed her
with a rough towel. Now I lift
the gown. But she holds up her palm—
there's a rip in the seam along

the shoulder. By gesture I suggest
we are in a place where almost
nothing is whole cloth, and anyway,
what's a little rip, it's nothing,

and the gown sweet and clean.
I hold it out to her, to smell.
Well. Possibly a ripped gown
is fine for me, I who have never

had to fight for water, beg
for food. Who come from a place,
where, when one gown goes,
there's another, a place of

illusion. And who am I, rich
bitch, to think Uma should take
what I offer. Uma knows
there are gowns without rips:

she wants one. She who consumes
no solid food, is incontinent,
too weak to sit up. I climb
to the roof, wander clean sheets,

sarongs, find a gown of whole
cloth. Go down, offer it
for Uma's inspection. Thus
my Lieutenant chalks up one more

victory, instructs me in poverty's
militancy. Without armor,
you turn warrior. I confess—
bless her—I love her brass.

Blind Bather

When the gods take away
    they also leave a gift. My lady
        likes to dawdle in the bath,
            soap herself everywhere
                she can reach, then look up—

though she can't see—ready to have me
    scrub her back. Track
        this lustrum as it extends
            beyond the tick of Sister
                Luke's grandfather clock

above that photograph
    of the steps of the Vatican,
        where, hand in hand,
            Mother Teresa and the Pope
                descend. Finally my lady's

ready to rinse. She likes me
    to dowse her. I fill the bowl,
        peals of water, arcing down
            from above. Now her skin's
                so clean its sheen

rings. Here, where there's
    a bed, plain food, no music,
        nothing electronic, no view
            of sky to measure the self
                by—if she could see—

still there's the sumptuous pleasure
    of spending a long time in vibratos
        of water, element eager
            to give up its treasure
                to each and every seeker.

Kalighat Hospice, Summer Solstice

Evening lowering, the lessening of light in its going
Leaves flickering in and out of slow dark's weave
Nuns gone up the stairs to prayer and dream
Only I am here, the last one leaving

Walking down this aisle, the women already sleeping
Shifting waves, each breath drifting into the others
And now, among the beds, a swell, sudden and rising
The girl, on her side, spine curled round her cancer

Gestalt of her body a swell in this ocean of breath
As though holding her hurt self out to the light
And flowing out from her spine a glowing fin
God energy, fanning out from the body

And if I should leave her alone, tell me
Something holds the wave together and disperses it
Something perfect, disfigured and divine
So be it, so it is   I am the one who lies down

Slides with her into the scintillant blur of electrons
Circling us the way gulls spiral over ocean
Streamers in air Wisp lengths of airborne cloud
Strands of fine linen torn by many hands

Wrappings for the dissolving body's winding
Ash   stargas   nebulous   drifting   ghostcloth
Parachute silks, thousands, spiraling around us
Circling   ritual of wrapping   shroudcloth

While somewhere else a place is prepared
How long can we float in this ceremony of shape
How long can she anchor in my material arms
Her hand on mine, asking my skin to speak

And what shall I say *Yes, you are   and are*
Yes you are going away before us
All of us going where you go across water
Our longing going before us where we follow

There is nothing to do, nowhere to go
I lie along her length, the length of my body open
Knowing with the porous wave of my body
The wave of the one who is going away

Is it now   Now a swell's soft bloom
Pushing the water up, water going above itself
Rising in a glide, now hugely above itself
Something perfect, disfigured and divine

This is the god rising, going out, tongues burning
The water burning   the water lit with flame
Up toward the vast, unfathomable light
Down toward the vast, unfathomable dark

I am the last one to give her water—
The last to lie beside her like a lover—
The last one she touches with her long fingers—
The one here now   The one from whom she goes

And like a swell's sheer falling to the wave's floor,
Long in its slow, suspended plunge,
she falls away   The waters' huge descending
now rising, closing over her head—

See the black bark going from shore, sliding her
out of the cells: soul cargo, shimmering away—
Leaving on the surface these flecks of foam
The trillion trillion bubbles bursting

And myself, here at the circling equator
Here at the zenith of the circling year
Afloat below the nuns' high singing
Afloat on the breath of the women sleeping

Afloat on dark, on sweat, afloat on loosening strands
of light   Who am I now: single syllable
Pouring of the blood's ferocious requiem unfurled
Another wave rolled open, holding the dead girl

Transfiguration

The blind talk of a way out. I see.
—Bertolt Brecht

The last day was a day of excrement—
on the sheets, sarongs messed with it,
every other woman needing a bedpan,
then you had to empty them, rinse

and begin again. I began over.
Washing another woman my mantram.
This is the way to the worms' home.
Soon it will be your turn.

The sun sank. Late light, huge,
diminuendoed toward black. The room
stank, though it was still the cathedral.
The beds were low, you had to kneel:

I dipped a handful of rag in a bowl,
watched the water gather in its threads.
Little by little the water filled it
to the lip with the shine of wetness.

IV: LOVE

Trinity: Tea for Three

Sister Ignatius and I drink tea. Below,
the bay. The Bombay sea is gray
slate. Late afternoon, and would you say
that's a storm

brewing? Or say the sea
is brown, light slung. Shimmering lung,
it breathes great fits and starts. Ignatius
takes sugar. We are talking

of our thrilling anger, how it is like
a great love. Sister, look:
there is languor in the sea,
even when it bares

its fangs. How it bangs the shore:
importunate sea, such slippery water!
Ours the langour of slippery angels,
our anger liquor, and we are

drunk with it. (Shall I say
this tangerine is sanguine?)
Now wind winds up a storm, unfurls
the curtain. One virgin,

one whore, yes, let it pour,
to be in the world is sinful, don't
shut the window. (Sister
has married herself to Christ,

but the monsoon sea does not
give a damn. And the tea cup's lip
is the thinnest
china.) The wind is breath,

breathing us. The armure of her habit
texture in my fingers. Many
the sanguine tangerines we've eaten,
many the many we've rocked

in the dark. God
himself is dark, brilliant,
terrible. Well
rounded. We have rocked him

as well: he will not strike us
dead. Instead, what seemed a storm
splits open,
lets down a fan

of light: we watch that fan
unfurl: his hand
pulling aside the veil
to look at us here. (A cheap

shot: is that what you
thought? Is the beautiful
more than you can
handle?) Sister Ignatius and I

are lovers. Drunk on the torn
moment, its radiant
rags. We love the broken things
of this world. Kiss

the broken bodies. Here, Sister,
take this sanguine section
of tangerine, bite in: while the light
fills us. And another thing:

Christ is our consort,
and the sea's an animal
turning over in its bed.
How many hands are there

in this world! Sister,
let me whisper in the whorl
of your ear: see where Christ
swears with us the anguine

vow. I swear Christ bows
before us: the sky a shout.
The sea is many pairs of hands
holding each other, crying out.

Carpe Diem: Time Piece

In the next seat the young man from Bangalore sleeps,
or so it seems. I dream, toss, lean—
do I?—into his shoulder. Or say his shoulder
slides—does it?—against mine. A woman reads
the *Times* across the aisle, and Big Spender sun
puts money on the Pacific. My breast, that heap

of wheat Solomon sang. Bangalore's heaped
hand, my breast a hill where swallows sleep
as though they've drunk some sweet elixir. Sun
burnishes the sea, I close my eyes, lean
into his long fingers. Listen, I've read
The Song. Eyes closed, it's like that. His shoulder,

armored, gleams: a buckler's brass. My shoulder
stakes the linen tent. Now conjure heap
of my belly, thicket of hair. (Later I'll read
Mary Oliver.) Years before I'd slept
with someone blind, my body braille. We lean
into our book. The text reads us. The sun

looks sideways at the sighing sea. The sun
looks on, our hands mouths. My hand shoulders
forward, looking for antelope, a leaning
slope. Cunning hunter, crossing the heaped
savannah of his lap. Afterward, sleep
is milky sweet. I've read Duras, I've read

Huang O, Rabindranath Tagore. I've read
the Tao, and David Bohm. Each day the sun
lays down its ultimatum. Be: don't sleep
away this blazing gift, your life. His shoulder,
my eyes, his eyes: we look our fill. That heap
of sea is called a swell. It's not who leans

on whom, not gender, not power. I've always leaned
toward earth, air, water. Fire. I read
the body's scripture, freely chose. A heap

of wheat, in scripture, is poetry. The sun
strokes the sea every day, and the slope of a shoulder
is lyric braille. A stewardess (she'd slept,

leaning on the steward's shoulder) brings us heaps
of rice. The woman sleeps beneath her *Times.*
Bangalore's work is watches. The sun reads braille.

Gem Inn, Kandy

This is the window in a wall of windows
in the room where we lay down beside the end
of summer. And this, like the pool of a gown
fallen on the floor, is the diva moon's
aria. This is the poem we read, liquid
by Tagore. This is the bolt lock on the door.

This is the bed made by sliding two beds
together. This is the hour where we spoke
a dialect we had not dared speak before.
And this is the scent of plumeria, redolent
on the air, sharp as rare metal. This
is the opening into the lair of an animal

and this is your hand, there. Here I sing
the recitative of everything we did together
in that room, in another country. Now my mouth
closed around silence: whom will it kiss? To whom
whisper? Tell me one thing sweeter than the whispering
of two friends, who have found each other
after long, diligent loneliness. I drink
from a glass half full of light, half full of dark.

Sapphics, Beginning with a Line
by Marilyn Hacker

"I would love my love, but my love is elsewhere"
and also beside me. What is this physics?
How has it come about that I am always
loved, I who was long

legged and lovely, but lonely so long? Left,
I imagined, like the last pear on the plate.
Though late, I've seen through the scrim of self hate, to
slow transformation

even I hadn't noticed, thinking the while
I was still the unloved one, when in fact, on
a cellular level, among electrons,
I was already

someone who is loved, she just doesn't know it.
And all through that time I was busy loving
the unloved—a student whose mother had died,
another bereft

of part of her body, her wailing clouding
the space between her and the rest of us, that
man who denied his own doubt, his crippled heart.
We don't understand

that this landscape we live in, these waves streaming
through matter and time (where stone's molten), water
a faster version of stone, and the trees are
some god's green ocean—

these waves which, as they move through us, move us,
waves we can't hold but which hold us, render us
one and the same moving thing we call this world.
Strange, how when we think

we're failing at the life we thought we wanted,
the life we have, now shining through that failure,

has become the one we looked for all along.
You are with me now

as the earth turns over into more darkness,
coming in this turning again and again
into light. So you and I, turning again
toward the other,

find we have come through dark, into a lit place
which doesn't stop moving us on into its
shadow, which broad, deeply moving space is now
the place we both are.

Homage to Pierre August Renoir

Leaving the museum at noon: the rain soaked street
a glittering scatter—Impressionism, a painter—
of subatomic particles, and I remember our bodies:
two strands of a necklace, one pearl, the beads of the other
amber of satinwood. Add moon across surf, a marbled
wave. Begin with a lover, and beyond, the world

is scintillant coruscations. Breathe in the world:
breath's a burnishing, though the shimmering street
opens on an alley's shattered glass. (On brick, the marbled
crayon scrawl: God made me.) Renoir's paintings
reveal it: light, and the light's longing. What other
longing could be this pure. We are porous bodies,

all of us one body, and when we leave the body,
we are still one. Behold the lit, wet world:
rainlight, windlight, the green light of flora, another
moment in a universe of moments, glorioso. In the street,
the millions pass. Alive as those stones the painter
plants, as light grows across them: burnished marbles

lit from within. Boys lean against the marble
facade, polishing a moment. I ride the body's
wave, not alone. In *Path in the forest* the painter
renders light a moving blur: this world's
impermanence. (I left you, the moonwashed street
tossed up a blind man, and I took the hand of The Other

like a lover.) Thanks for giving us another
chance, and another and another. One moment the marbled
chiaroscuro of leaf light dapples a street
and then it's gone, leaving those of us with bodies
bereft—until the next moment. Kiss this world
goodby: zero: here it comes again. Great paintings

render dark and light one longing. In the painting
Seated Bather, ground/figure resemble each other.
You were once my moment, as I was yours, in that world

where all down its length the sand strung shore, in marbled
light, was the sea's. Now, in the fullness of the body,
wordy and sensuous, I descend to the street:

the street steams. Time, in those paintings, unfurls.
Marble is slowed down light and doesn't last.
Wherever you are, friend, is the body of the world.

Treatise on Beauty, Fairness, Honesty, and Possession

My grandmother told me there was a reason for everything,
God had his reasons. A reason some people had to be
crippled, a reason some had to wear secondhand clothes.
But now here you are, and you are beautiful
for no reason, here where we worship Beauty, that bitch—

you can bang your forehead in the dirt and she won't bat
an eyelash, you can crawl and she may still choose
not to be pleased. We worship her, I worship her
in you, you are my golden calf, and though God
does not approve of idols, he gave you everything,

and others practically nothing at all. Nor
will the ugly inherit the earth. The beautiful have already
bought up the property. I cannot approve this,
but when I look at you, I think God risked his reputation
for this truth: there can be no honesty

without painful choices. I choose
painful choices. It isn't fair, but God has always
been unfair. We don't like it, but somebody's
got to do it. I do it now, without the slightest
remorse. Scrupulously I compare you with the others

as they go by. You are beautiful, and the others
not very, and that is all there is to it. Anyone honest
will admit this. I admit I choose you
because you're beautiful and for no other reason:
you, with skin the color of satinwood, gleaming,

and, while you worship me, mine.

Eden of Water

Know where you came from. Know
the sea: garden where water
grows like grass. Now from this elemental bath
she rises—Eve, Alpha, Omega, woman,
a lustrum, protean perfume, fluid, poured
over bone. But briefly. Eyes, salt, hair:

the mineral earth turns, and her hair
burns. Ask her what she knows
with certainty: the gulf stream, poured
into cold, churning forward, warming the distances, a watery
unfurling: pure energy, orgasmic, womanly,
saying it over and over again. We bathe

in time, as the seal turning in the curl, bathes
his way home in a net of moments. Her hair
grows long, and the second comes over and over, a woman
faithful to herself. Know you cannot say no,
Adam, son of the fathers parting the waters
for an instant only. You, like the rest of us, poured

into flesh. We exist as instants—grains—pouring
through the hour glass, this bath
of translucence, water itself washed clean. Water
our medium, the body—eyes, salt, hair—
a momentary blur. Flesh aquifer. She knows
granite's an illusion, Brancusi's man and woman

mouth to mouth in stone. That other woman,
the Venus of Willendorf: liquid resplendence, poured
into a stone jar. Eve, tidal, knows
no boundaries. Solids at her feet sieve into a bath
of sand. Adam—here for an instant—black hair
everywhere on his body. Eve is all eyes. Then water

engulfs us, the earth turns. The waters
of the deep take a thousand years to rise. Womanly
and wet, the seconds' ablutions, Eve's hair

down to her knees. As sun pours
into dark, honor the damp instants. Not bathos
but glory. Water is God's womb. Know

your origins: know the amniotic, that hairy
place where the waters of Paradise pour into the earthly
compass. Sea's a woman bathing herself.

Poem for Extraordinary Day

When I've worked hard and am done, I go out from that place
and look up at the sky. It comes to me then
how substantial good work is, how it
empties and fills us, the way birds
wheel across clouds, filling and emptying and filling

the heavens. If there's grass, I lie down and look up
a long time. Then I walk home, slow like the light
going slowly
into another form

of itself. I come where you sit
in the solemnity of evening, and we watch it
get dark, taking our time, then sitting down
at the table, eating something,
noticing all the little things
about each other
we like to remember, and talking
of all that has happened
with that slow calm that comes at the end of a day

like the calm in a body of water
nothing disturbs. In that leisure
I look at you
for the pure sake of drinking in what I see,
until we move closer, touch each other
and go on touching, coming finally
to the end of what resembles,
when you're thirsty, a drink of cold

water. And when we have done these things,
I will be full, and it will time then
to flick off the light
and let everything go—
because I will have known the immeasurable pleasure
of filling a day
with the good things there are to do,

and I will be weary and utterly
unable
to tell any boundary
between myself, you, and the things of this world.

Notes

Ghazal 5: "Pain with the thousand teeth...":William Watson.

Ghazal 6: The first quotation is from Whitman, the second from Edna St.Vincent Millay.

Ghazal 13: "As I would not be a slave...":Abraham Lincoln. The italicized quotation is from Rumi.

Rite: The quotation is from Isa Upanishad,Yeats's translation.

Ghazal 15: The quote is from Rumi.

Ghazal 16: The quote is from the Tao.

Ghazal 17: The poet is Mary Oliver.The quote is from Rumi.